TO: KAREN RUBINO

M000024284

JUST A MARINE

AULTON KOHN
GUNNERY SERGEANT, USMC (RET)

All rights reserved. No part of this book shall be reproduced or transmitted in any form or by any means, electronic, mechanical, magnetic, photographic including photocopying, recording or by any information storage and retrieval system, without prior written permission of the publisher. No patent liability is assumed with respect to the use of the information contained herein. Although every precaution has been taken in the preparation of this book, the publisher and author assume no responsibility for errors or omissions. Neither is any liability assumed for damages resulting from the use of the information contained herein.

Neither the United States Marine Corps nor any other component of the Department of Defense has approved, endorsed or authorized this product.

Copyright © 2011 by Aulton Kohn

ISBN 0-7414-6857-3

Printed in the United States of America

Published October 2011

INFINITY PUBLISHING
1094 New DeHaven Street, Suite 100
West Conshohocken, PA 19428-2713
Toll-free (877) BUY BOOK
Local Phone (610) 941-9999
Fax (610) 941-9959
Info@buybooksontheweb.com
www.buybooksontheweb.com

DEDICATION

Dedicated to my mother and father: Jerry & Elizabeth Kohn,
and to my many family members, along with the countless friends and
co-workers that have touched my life in so many special ways.

TABLE OF CONTENTS

PREFACE

The year was 1968 and the war in Vietnam was hot and heavy. I was 19 years old and had received my draft notice to report for my induction physical to enter into the U.S. Army. Now this young man was not motivated about going into the Army. I had quite a few relatives that had gone into the Army, and my father was in the Navy. What I really wanted was to wear those blue trousers with the red stripe which belong to a Marine.

Aulton Kohn
Gunnery Sergeant
USMC (ret)

U.S. MARINE CORPS
CAREER SUMMARY

1968	*Entered the Marine Corps, and deployed to Vietnam*
1969	*Military Policeman, Camp Lejuene, North Carolina*
1972	*Patrolman, Kaneohe Bay, Hawaii*
1975	*Patrol Supervisor/SWAT team leader, Camp Pendleton, California*
1976	*Recruiting Duty, Kansas City, Kansas*
1978	*Patrol Supervisor, Camp Lejeune, North Carolina*
1982	*Training Non Commission officer-in-charge, Iwakuni, Japan*
1983	*Patrol Supervisor, Camp Pendleton, California*
1986	Correctional Duty Warden, Iwakuni, Japan
1987	Watch Commander, Marine Corps air Station, Beaufort, South Carolina
1990	Training Non Commission Officer in Charge, Iwakuni, Japan
1991	Service Chief, Marine Corps Air Station, Beaufort, S.C./Retired from the Marine Corps
1991	Bowling center mechanic, Parris Island, South Carolina
2000	Information receptionist, Museum, Parris Island, South Carolina
2011	FULLY RETIRED

PERSONAL DECORATIONS

1. Purple Heart
2. Combat Action Ribbon
3. Presidential Unit Citation
4. Good Conduct Medal
5. National Defense Medal
6. Vietnam Service Medal
7. Sea Service Deployment Ribbon
8. Republic of Vietnam Cross of Gallantry
9. Vietnam Campaign Medal
10. Humanitarian Service Medal

U.S. MARINE CORPS RECRUIT DEPOT
PARRIS ISLAND, SOUTH CAROLINA

Simply put, Marine Corps Recruit Depot (MCRD), Parris Island has the mission of enlisting and training the men and women willing to give of themselves to become a part of the United States Marine Corps.

More than 20,000 new Marines leave Parris Island each year after graduating from recruit training. They will continue on to Marine Corps Base, Camp Lejeune, North Carolina for Marine Combat Training, Before going on to their Military Occupational Specialty School to be trained in the duties they will perform as members of the world's most elite fighting force-The United States Marine Corps.

The training objective is to instill self-discipline and confidence; high moral standards; basic military knowledge and individual skills; a warrior spirit; physical fitness and wellness as a way of life; pride, respect and love of Corps and Country.

Upon arriving at MCRD, Parris Island, S.C. I was placed at the receiving barracks for forming. After enough recruits had arrived for a platoon, we were assigned to Platoon 395, Third Recruit Training Battalion.

We were formally introduced to the drill instructors who had the task of transforming us into Marines; Senior Drill Instructor Staff Sergeant R.E. Shoemaker; Assistant Drill Instructor Staff Sergeant J.R. Phillps, Assistant Drill Instructor Sergeant Holzapfel and Assistant Drill Instructor Sergeant B.L. Bernier.

I didn't know it at the time, but one drill instructor, Sergeant Bernier, would have a major impact on my career in the Marine Corps and well beyond my retirement. From the time I met him, I knew without a doubt that he was a certified nut. He talked about everyone in your family and start calling me a f*&^%ing, worm. Twice more during my career, Sergeant Bernier and I crossed paths. The second time was on Okinawa, Japan and the last time was at the Staff Non-Commissioned Officer Academy at Quantico, VA. I was a student and he was the company First Sergeant

After my retirement from the Marine Corps in August 1991, I lost contact with First Sergeant Bernier. If I could, I would like to see him once again to tell him thanks for everything he taught me about being a man, and the impact he had on my life.

After enlisting into the Marine Corps, I convinced myself that before I finished boot camp, the war in Vietnam would be over, but I was wrong. After completing boot camp I received orders to attend the Infantry Training Regiment (ITR) at Camp Geiger for further infantry training. The base was located at Camp Lejeune, N.C.

The male Marines going into an infantry military occupation specialty (MOS) attended the School Of Infantry. After graduation from there, these Marines will be assigned to their first permanent duty station. Male Marines with a non-infantry MOS also go to Camp Geiger but take part in Marine Combat Training. MCT reinforces the basic Marine combat skills learned in recruit training. Following MCT, Marines attends MOS schools to learn the job they are expected to perform in the Marine Corps.

Once again I had convinced myself that after I completed ITR the war in Vietnam would be over, but once again I was wrong. I received my orders to report for duty in the Republic of Vietnam.

Parris Island
The Birthplace Of The Enlisted Marines

Parris Island is widely-known today as the birthplace for enlisted Marines. Males from the east of the Mississippi River and females from the entire country and its territories. But the island has a relationship with leathernecks that span over a century and a military history dating before the birth of the Corps in 1775.

The French were the first Europeans to build a military installation on Parris Island. French explorer Jean Ribaut fortified a small garrison on Parris Island in 1562. The position, names Charlesforte, was thought by Ribaut to be the perfect place to sneak attack vessels carrying gold and silver owned by the Spanish, who claimed the entire east coast of the United States as their own. Charlesforte, however, was quickly crumbling at the hands of mutiny.

The Spanish, fearing any return of the French to the valuable seaport, established Santa Helena on the island. This settlement was also disbanded, this time by the conquering English forces, who, colonized South Carolina and laid claim to Parris Island.

Alexander Parris, for whom the island is named, was a treasurer of South Carolina who purchased the island in the early 1700's. Although he owned Parris Island, he actually never lived there.

It was during the Civil war that Marines would first set foot on Parris Island. Victory in the battle for Port Royal was a necessary in the eyes of the Union Leaders, and Parris Island was where the Union Naval forces anchored and set up camp during the battle.

After the island was formally dedicated, U.S. Naval Station, Port Royal on 26 June, 1891, the permanent relationship between the Marine Corps and Parris Island had begun. In 1898, Marines trained for war against Spain, and in 1909, a Marine Officer school was opened here. In fact, Parris Island temporarily served as a temporary recruit training facility and a disciplinary barracks before World War 1 necessitated a permanent facility for recruit training.

Parris Island would see 46,602 Marines trained for that war- in which Marines fought so valiantly that the Germans they battled nicknamed them 'Devil Dogs."

The Depot was permanently connected to the mainland by causeway, which officially opened on Christmas day, 1929. Before this, the main transportation to and from Parris Island was by small boats and barges.

In World War 11 and every war since, the Marines again and again distinguished themselves on countless battlefields after receiving training at Parris Island. Parris Island has been "where the difference begins" for more than a million enlisted Marines. Only an island with such unique history in war and peace could be the home for Marines who continuously shine throughout those time

THE DRILL INSTRUCTOR
MAKER OF MARINES

Throughout generations of Marines, stories are passed on from one Marine to another about how hard recruit training was.

It is said no Marine ever forgets the names of his or her drill instructors and how demanding they were during recruit training. They are the ones responsible for the transformation of raw recruits into the "FEW, THE PROUD, THE MARINES.

The drill instructor must accomplish the mission of providing the Marine Corps with basically trained Marines.

Everything about training recruits brings a sense of pride for being the one responsible for transforming raw individuals into The Few, The Proud, The Marines.

Those Marines directly involved in the recruit training process must always remember that they bear the ultimate responsibility for the welfare of recruits in their charge. The Marine Corps has placed great trust in selecting those Marines responsible for carrying out the task of turning raw recruits into Marines. Those results are seen weekly when those recruits are transformed into the world's finest fighting force.

The Drill Instructor Pledge

These recruits are entrusted to my care. I will train them to the best of my ability. I will develop them into smartly disciplined, physically fit, basically trained Marines, thoroughly indoctrinated in love of Corps and country. I will demand of them, and demonstrate by my own example, the highest standards of personal conduct, morality, and professional skill.

The End Of The Beginning

It is the end, and it is the beginning.

The end- of approximately three months of rigorous training, three months of being away from home and three months of blood, sweat and tears.

The beginning- of a new life for a person who has now earned the title of one of the world's elite, a U.S. Marine.

Pvt. Kohn

PLATOON 395

THIRD RECRUIT BATTALION   M. C. R. D., PARRIS ISLAND, S. C.
SGT.K.H.HOLZAPFEL   SSGT.J.R.PHILLIPS   SSGT.R.E.SHOEMAKER   SSGT.W.H.CLARK
                        GRADUATED 9 SEPTEMBER 1968

GRADUATION

Recruit training comes to a long-awaited end during the graduation ceremony where recruits are transformed into Marines, the title they have worked hard to earn.

Traditionally, recruits families and friends visit Parris Island the day before graduation to see their recruit during their liberty. It is then that recruits get to see their family and friends for the first time since arriving aboard Parris Island.

During this time, recruits and their families can visit the barracks and various other areas of the Depot to see demonstrations and displays.

On graduation day, families can attend the Morning Colors Ceremony prior to graduation. The hour-long ceremony begins at 0800 at the headquarters building.

Now, after completing three mentally and physically challenging phases of training spread out over 13 weeks, the recruits are ready to march across the parade deck.

The ceremony begins with the graduating companies marching onto the Peatross Parade Deck, while being led by the Parris Island Marine Band. Upon stopping and establishing proper alignment, each series officially reports in.

Next, an invocation is given by one of the Depot's Navy Chaplains, followed by an address by the Battalion Commander. He or she will be the first person to address the graduates as Marines. Following the address, each of the platoon's honor graduates are awarded the Commanding General's Medal and certificate of commendation for being chosen the most outstanding recruit in their platoon.

Then the entire formation is marched for a pass-in-review past the grand stands, where family and friends are watching the ceremony. During the pass-in-review, the guest of honor observes the graduating platoons as they march by.

At the conclusion of the ceremony, each of the platoon's guidon is retired. The guidon is a small flag bearing the platoon's number and is a symbol of their spirit, dedication, teamwork and unit identity. Then, the band will play a selection that recruits have come to know and love.... The Marine's Hymn.

Finally, the senior drill instructors issue the dismissal to their platoons, and the ceremony and recruit training is over.

New Marines leave recruit training with tangible items such as a new wardrobe and a new physical appearance, but what they have also gained are the intangible traits of Honor, Courage, and Commitment---- items which every Marine holds dear in their heart.

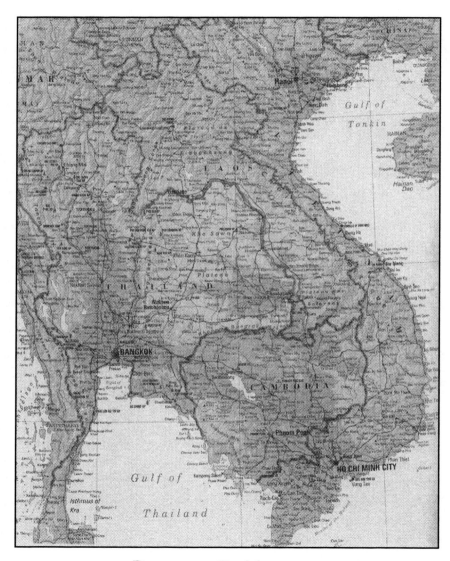

REPUBLIC OF VIETNAM

Vietnam is country on the eastern side of the Indochinese Peninsula in Southeast Asia. It is bounded on the north by China, on the west by Laos and Cambodia, on the east by the China Sea, and on the southwest by the Gulf of Thailand. Vietnam has three historic regions, Tonkin in the north, Annam in the center, and Cochin China in the south.

In 1945 a Communist-led nationalist movement known as the Vietminh proclaimed the nation's independence as the Democratic Republic of Vietnam. In the Indochina war, which began in 1946, the Vietminh guerrilla Army drove the French out of the peninsula.

In 1954 a French-Vietminh agreement that ended the war partitioned Vietnam at about the 17th parallel, with the area to the north under Vietminh control and the area to the south under an anti-Communist government backed by the United States. The partition was meant to be temporary, but planned elections to reunify Vietnam were never held because of South Vietnam and U.S. objections. The northern part became the Democratic Republic of Vietnam, or North Vietnam and the southern part became the Republic of Vietnam, or South Vietnam.

Its capital was Saigon (now Ho Chi Minh City). Both parts of Vietnam were devastated during the Vietnam War, which began in the late 1950's as a Communist-led rural insurgency in South Vietnam, grew in the 1960's into major war involving all of Vietnam and engaging more than half million troops from the United States, and ended in 1975 with the victory over the Communists. On July 2, 1976 the two parts of the country were officially reunited as the Socialist Republic of Vietnam.

Upon arriving in Vietnam and landing in Saigon was my first taste of combat, with incoming rounds. While we were deplaning on the tarmac. A Marine informed us we had better take cover in the nearest bunker because of the incoming rounds. It was at that time when it hit me I have finally been put in harm's way. In the next few days I was assigned to the 9th Marines Regiment in the 3rd Marine Division, Alpha Company, 1st Battalion 9th Marines which was known as The Walking Dead.

KOHN & CAMPBELL

THE DEAD WALK AMONG US

Upon being assigned to the 1ˢᵗ Battalion 9ᵗʰ Marines, a unit that eventually sustained the highest casualty rate of any unit in the Vietnam War, earning them the nickname "The Walking Dead." There are many stories as to how they got that name, but I don't know which one is true.

While I might not know the exact origin, but began to understand the definition when, just two month into my tour in Vietnam, the 36 man patrol which I was a member of was ambushed by the North Vietnamese Army. I was one of only two men to live through the attack.

The other surviving Marine, Lance Corporal Alonzo Campbell and I took stock of our surroundings and slowly made our way back to camp, a 58-day journey through the jungles of Vietnam. In addition to eating wild berries, roots of trees, and drinking from stagnant pools of water, we shot, killed and ate a monkey. Any apprehension about this was overcome by our survival instincts. We did whatever we had to do to stay alive.

We eventually spotted a unit of Green Berets, their figures looming larger than John Wayne. Upon making contact and explaining what happen, the Green Berets provided us with a helicopter ride back to our camp. On the first day back we were debriefed. On the second day we were given a steak dinner, and on the third, with replacements, we found ourselves back in the jungles of Vietnam.

I was later shot in the leg and hit in the arm, receiving a Purple Heart Medal for service during the war. Those exploits earned me a certain amount of fame, especially in military circles, but I still just consider myself "Just a Marine."

I later switched my mos from the infantry to the military police where I finally got the opportunity to wear those blue trousers with red stripes. In 1990 was transferred to the Marine Corps Air Station in Iwakuni Japan, where I decided to retired in August 1991 after being denied my request to serve in Operation Desert Storm.

"I told them that I'd rather retire than not go to Iraq, so I was transferred to (Marine Corps Air Station in Beaufort, South Carolina for retirement

Wisegraver & Feddlers

Hunter, Noland, & Kohn

Kohn, Wisegraver, Feddlers,
and Hunter

Kohn & Noland

AULTON KOHN, GYSGT, USMC
PERSONALITY OF THE WEEK APRIL 8, 2005

Thirty years and still going strong... Retired Marine stays active in Marine Corps community. After more than 22 years with the Marine Corps, his pride is still as strong as ever. He has experienced the anguish of patrolling the jungles of Vietnam in search of unseen enemies and was one of the first permanent military policemen in the Marine Corps. Now he shares these experiences with hundreds of visitors, recruits and new Marines each week at the Parris Island Marine Corps Depot Museum, with his Marine Corps baseball cap and old unit insignia worn proudly.

Aulton Kohn, information receptionist at the Parris Island Museum spent 22 years and six months in the Marine Corps and retired as a Gunnery Sergeant. Although he came to love this brotherhood of warriors, it was not always his intention to be a part of it for more than two decades.

Now, at the Parris Island Museum, Kohn grew up in a family of military tradition. My father was in the Navy and his brother, among many other relatives, served with the Army. Kohn had opted for college instead of going into the service but that plan changed as the needs for troops in Vietnam began to rise. One by one, he watched his friend get drafted into the Army so Kohn came to the realization that he would soon be following in their footsteps.

By my father being in the Navy, so I knew that was out; and all my relatives, including my brother, went into the Army, so I knew that was out, Kohn said. "When I got my induction letter to be drafted into the Army, I decided the Marine Corps, was it."

Kohn recalled memories of seeing Marines guarding the Navy bases and remembered how sharp their uniforms looked.

"I always wanted to wear those blue trousers with the red stripe," he said. "I figured if I had to go into the military it might as well be with the best."

His choice of service went against the grain of his family but they were all still pretty proud of his decision although the inter-service rivalry was still there.

It was all in good fun," he said with a smile. "My father used to call me a jarhead and I would call him a squid and would tell my brother that the Army was just advanced Boy Scouts."

But with all joking aside, Kohn's newfound life in the military led him to a position as an infantryman, a job that would lead him straight to war.

"Vietnam was my first duty station," said Kohn, where his unit was Alpha Company, 1st Battalion, 9th Marines, known as "The Walking Dead."

After his two-year mark in the infantry, Kohn was selected for Military Police duty. At the time, the military occupational specialty did not exist within the Marine Corps so Marines from different units had to be temporarily assigned to this duty to fill its ranks, which was (FAP) Fleet Assistance Program. Eventually, Kohn found himself back with the infantry, but after a long march that he throught would kill him. Kohn made a call to see if he would be able to return to the Military Police. He called the Master Gunnery Sergeant to see if he could get him transferred back.

By this time, the Military Police field had been established as a permanent job field and the Master Gunnery Sergeant did end up getting Kohn back with them, but it was for good.

"He throught I wanted to change my MOS to stay over there permanently. I stayed as a Military Policeman for the next twenty years and six months."

As a MP, Kohn spent time aboard Marine Corps Base, Camp LeJeune, North Carolina, Marine Corp Base, Camp Pendleton, California, and Marine Corps Air Station, Iwakuni, Japan to name a few. Kohn have held the billets of Watch Commander, Patrol Supervisor, Swat Team Leader. The Swat Team that led to one of his most memorable moments as a Military Policeman.

"Usually, when the SWAT team is called out, everything else has broken down. When you call out the SWAT team, somebody is going to get hurt… they don't get called out for every little thing."

At this time, Kohn was station at MCB Camp Pendleton, California, and the reason they were called out was because a Marine was shooting at cars as they passed his barracks room.

"While he was at the window, my team broke the door down and each of us rushed in with our weapons drawn and pointing at him. He was instructed that if he didn't drop his weapon we would shoot him. All of a sudden he came too his senses and dropped it."

Following his tour of duty in the Marine Corp, after over 22 years Kohn retired and had an opportunity to work for the Beaufort Sheriff's Office but, after a brief stay, he decided otherwise.

After he passed up the career in Law Enforcement, Kohn looked back towards the Marine Corps for a job and soon settled into a position aboard Parris Island as a mechanic with the bowling center. After eight years in the position, a better position at the Museum opened and he jumped at the opportunity

Kohn has been with the Museum for nearly four years now and keeps his ties with the Marine Corps and its youth as strong as ever. He is a member of the "Once a Marine, Always a Marine" program and is also the Commanding Officer of the Parris Island Young Marines Program. A program he says allows him to not only teach Honor, Courage, and Commitment but lets him teach through his experiences—experiences that have been forged in the furnaces of the Marine Corps for the past three decades.

LANCE CORPORAL, JUSTIN J. SHEMANSKI
STAFF WRITER/THE BOOT, PARRIS ISLAND SOUTH CAROLINA

Aulton Kohn, GySgt, USMC
Living Legend Retires From Depot

After serving 22 years as an active duty Marine, retired Gunnery Sergeant and "Walking Dead" survivor Aulton Kohn began working aboard Marine Corps Recruit Depot Parris Island in 1991.

The Jacksonville, Florida, native first worked at the bowling center. He then found his place as a museum technician at the Parris Island Museum several years later, where he stayed for 12 years before retiring on 31 May 2011.

His duties at the museum consisted of guiding tours for visitors aboard the depot, coordinating with the Parris Island community relations department for special visits, teaching Marine Corps history to museum patrons and sharing Marine Corps history through the Share the Legacy program.

Most people – Marines and civilian Marines alike- know him as a very jovial individual who almost never turns down the opportunity to help a friend of stranger

Kohn, while working at the museum, had the opportunity to meet thousands of people each year – some more recognizable than others.

"One thing about working there was the number of interesting people who visited the museum. Kohn said, referring to fellow retirees, veterans and active duty Marines.

While in the Corps, Kohn was a military policeman by trade, but filled a few different roles during his career. Through out his career he was a recruiter in Kansa City, Kansas and the Marine Corps special reaction team leader in California.

Kohn also served as the brig duty warden aboard Marine Corps Air Station, Iwakuni, Japan as a Staff Sergeant.

"It was an experience," he said laughing. "I was always the duty warden because there was only one warden." Although it is Kohn's second time retiring, he will still put in a few hours as a volunteer to conduct tours for the depot visitors after a long awaited vacation.

"For now, I'm just going to take it easy and travel," he said. :Most of my days will be spent doing a lot of fishing. Kohn's legacy will stay at the museum in the form of an exhibit about the famed "Walking Dead" of Vietnam. Kohn, a private first class at the time, was assigned to the 3rd platoon, Alpha Company, 1st Battalion, 9th Marine Regiment in 1969.

The platoon's mission was to locate and ambush the enemy, but on their fifth night of patrol they were taken by surprise by an L-shaped ambush. Kohn and one other Marine, Lance Corporal Alfonzo Campbell, were the only survivors of the attack.

"They let loose with everything they had on us," Kohn explain, "They fired rockets, small arms and grenades. We walked right into it.

After the attack, Kohn and Campbell took their first steps on their famed excursion through the jungles of Vietnam. They survived by drinking stagnant water and eating berries, bugs and the meat of a monkey they shot and killed.

The duo eventually spotted a group of Army Special Forces soldiers on their 58 day which was Kohn's 19th birthday.

After getting a ride in a helicopter back to the rear area, the first day back was spent in de-briefing, then we was treated to a steak dinner on the second day, and the third day with replacements we were headed back out once again.

After 42 years of serving the Marine Corps in one capacity or another, Kohn gladly offers his wisdom and advice for a successful career.

"If there's one thing I've learned, It's is to enjoy your job," he said with a smile. "If you can enjoy what you do, everything will turn out all right.

LANCE CORPORAL JAVARRE GLANTON
STAFF WRITER/ THE BOOT/10 JUNE 2011

MEDITERRANEAN CRUISE

September, 1979/February, 1980

MEDITERRANEAN DEPLOYMENTS

USS SAGINAW LST # 1188

One of the principal elements of our National Defense is our forward military strategy. The United States is essentially an overseas oriented country due mainly to our politics, geography, economics, and cultural heritage. To maintain the high standard of living we enjoy and to take advantage of the security the oceanic distance affords, requires that we possess the ability and creditability to positively influence international affairs. In the event of conflict we must be able to engage and defeat the enemy far from America's shores. One of the requirements of the forward strategy requires overseas deployment of units such as the USS SAGINAW in the Mediterranean Sea.

Upon arriving in the Mediterranean, we took part in "Display Determination 79," which is a NATO exercise designed to demonstrate and refine NATO's capability to deploy forces rapidly to the Mediterranean and to project power ashore to reinforce NATO's Southern Region. The operation was conducted in Sardinia and Saros Bay Turkey.

The first liberty port we pulled into was La Spezia, Italy, which proved a convenient springboard for day trips to the larger and better known cities of GENOA, PISA, AND FLORENCE, ITALY. A opportunity I didn't pass up on.

After a few days in Italy, we departed for our next port which was Toulon, France. It was a familiar place to many crewmembers and Marines alike, having visited it on a previous Mediterranean Deployment.

Toulon is a leading naval arsenal of France with a history dating back to the Phoenicians. During World War 11 the French scuttled their fleet anchored there to prevent it from falling into German hands. In Toulon we had the services of the USO which helped us with anything and everything, from monetary exchange to sightseeing. Many did take advantage of the latter insofar as Toulon lies between Marseille, another famous seaport on the west, and Monaco, home of Monte Carlo, to the east. A few determined individuals like myself, even made the long trek to Paris, 410 miles to the north. After five days in Toulon the Saginaw pulled out and steamed east towards our next port visit in Venice, Italy.

In Venice the Marines participated in cross training, with the host, the Italian Amtrack Brigade, whose function is river assaults along their river borders.

During our five day excursion the Marines of both nations ate, drank, slept and entertained each other. We spent Thanksgiving together in the field playing football, Frisbee, and cards.

Venice was probably the most unique, if not the most beautiful of the port cities visited; a place most people lamented not having the time to see more of. As we approached her from the sea the distinctive architecture of this ancient city rose sharply upon us, giving it the appearance of floating on the water. The Saginaw spent one day in Venice and then pulled out for two days of joint operations with the Italian Navy, after which we enjoyed two more days of liberty in this canal-wrought city. Cars are unknown there; instead boats and the traditional gondolas ply the intricate and numerous waterways which divide the city into a group of 122 islets. A side from the boats, one gets around via bridges and narrow walkways. Home of St. Mark's Cathedral and Square. Many sailors and Marines hand-fed the pigeons which flock there. Holding out their peanut-filled hands, they soon found themselves covered with the birds.

What would a Mediterranean Cruise be without pulling into Naples, Italy? Familiar to many, "different" to some but big enough for all, Naples is a city apart from any city in Italy. It is a place where traffic lights long ago lost their power to control the madcap and often frightening driving patterns; where the "Napolitanos" diligently go their own way in everything from language to politics, where any of God's creations (from beer cans to entire cows) can be seen floating in the bay on an average day. It is also a city which harbors the most comfortable and capable USO in the Mediterranean, as well as being a stepping-off point for jaunts to nearby Rome, the resurrected Pompeii (smothered in lava and volcanic ash 1900 years ago) and the jewel-like isle of Capri, a hydrofoil ride away. A Mediterranean deployment may be wrought with uncertainties and last-minute changes of plans, but in the midst of what the sailors see as a grand confusion at times, Naples stands out as the one fact of Mediterranean deployment life, whether it be for a cool beer in an out of the way bar or a bicycle ride along the extensive waterfront

Barcelona, Spain for Christmas was an idea which seemed to please everybody. Arriving there late Christmas Eve, the SAGINAW pulled in, in time to let many sailors and

Marines go ashore whose families had flown in for the holidays. As New Year's Eve approached many of us got caught up in the local festivities and celebrated the advent of 1980 with the people of this beautiful city.

Barcelona lies on the northeast coast of Spain and is the Capital of the Province of Catalonia, a region set apart from the rest of Spain in political tone, language and customs. Barcelona is representative of both the old and new in Europe, with narrow, winding streets enmeshing the great Cathedral in the old section and broad, handsome boulevards in the modern part. The Ramblas is a long tree-lined avenue leading from the waterfront into the heart of the city, along which local artisans cluster shoulder-to-shoulder to display and sell their handicrafts. From Barcelona some individuals as myself, made our way north to Andorra, the smallest of all countries strung high in the Pyrenees between France and Spain, finding a white Christmas after all.

The German writer-philosopher Goethe wrote that to have seen Italy without having seen Sicily is not to have seen Italy at all. Taking the great man's cue, The SAGINAW paid a port visit to Messina, just across from the "toe" of mainland Italy. Sailors and Marines consumed the best pizza of the cruise here and in great full return SAGINAW's own "Brand X" band offered the townsfolk a pier side concert.

The city is low, sprawling and rather quiet, with an ever-curious people who could always be found milling about the waterfront looking the SAGINAW over. One day was set aside for open house and the people descended on the ship en masse, remaining on board through the evening.

Northeastern Sicily is dominated by the great and snowy Mt. Etna, the largest active volcano in Europe, and to which a group of sailors and Marines headed for an enjoyable and relatively accident –free ski trip. The volcano itself was benevolent and kept its cool throughout the adventure.

The last and most cosmopolitan of our port visits was Palma, Spain. The weather was just right and so were the people, who came from all over Europe.

Palma is situated on the island of Mallorca, the largest of the Balearic island group. Known as the Pearl of the Mediterranean, it is a place of mountains, unspoiled beaches and much in the way of entertainment. There seemed to be something for everyone here, and weather it was hitting the clubs, horseback riding, shopping or just strolling about, more than a few of us considered Palma to be the best liberty port of the cruise, making it an appropriate climax of events.

As The SAGINAW was returning to port in Morehead City, North Carolina to off load the Marines. I found myself thinking of the many different foreign countries and cities that I had visited and the many friends that I had made. The different customs, languages, food and how much everyone was so friendly in trying to communicate with each other.

The one thing that I really learned from this 6 month Mediterranean Cruise was that you might not have understood their language of the food you were trying but music and a SMILE will bring down any barriers

I also got too spend 30 days in NORWAY, in which I got the opportunity to visit cities of Brekstad, Trondheim, and Oslo, Norway. Some of the people there is still my friends today. We keep in contact by letters and e-mailing.

I've been station in Japan on many occasions and while there I got the opportunity to visit China and the famous Great Wall of China

I have visited many foreign countries and traveled through-out the United States it was made possible because I wanted to be JUST A MARINE.

The Young Marines Of Parris Island

As the Commanding Officer of the Young Marines of Parris Island, I used the program as a outlet to praise the ideals and instill the values of the Marine Corps.

The Young Marine program was formed in 1958 in Waterbury, Conn. And is designed for kids from eight years of age through completion of high school. It includes classroom instruction, physical training, and participants wear uniforms and earn rank. Besides weekly meetings, the Young Marines complete 13 weeks of recruit training or "boot camp" on Saturdays for three hours each Saturday.

The best benefit of leading the Young Marines is being able to see the positive outcomes in those who complete the program. Seeing these kids grow in their self-esteem and confidence you can really see them benefit from the structure and accountability.

Though a decorated veteran and survivor of unimaginable circumstances, I will remain " Just a Marine" whose role was trying to help shape the next generations of leaders.

I just like to see the great changes in the kid's attitudes and know that the Young Marine program did them good.

After leading the Young Marines of Parris Island for seven years I decided to resign and start doing other things that peaked my interested.

Retirement

Upon retirement I decided to stay in the Beaufort area because of its strong military community; plus, I like the fishing and the shrimping.

After passing up a career in law enforcement, I accepted a position at the Parris Island Bowling Center as the mechanic for the next eight years. A Civil Service position at the Parris Island Museum opened and I was hired. It gave me plenty of opportunities to practice my favorite hobby of talking with people about the Marine Corps.

The majority of people that visit Parris Island have heard about the things the Marine Corps has done throughout our history, but they don't know all the facts. I give first-hand knowledge from my time in the Marine Corps that help them relate to what we're all about.

On 31 May 2011, I decided to retire from Civil Service at the Parris Island Museum. After 42 years of serving the Marine Corps and Civil Service in one capacity or another my parting wisdom and advice for a successful career:

Enjoy your job, always have a great attitude and. Smile. If you can do that then everything will turn out alright.

FAMILY AND FRIENDS COMMENTS

MISS FREDRIKA JONES
PLACE OF BIRTH: JACKSONVILLE, FLORIDA
DAUGHTER

You gain strength and experience by everyday living. My dad has inspired a lot of people in his life and has touched so many hearts. Through the years he has been a mentor to the youth in the community. His happiness was the key to his success.

MR. AULTON KOHN JR.
PLACE OF BIRTH: CAMP PENDLETON, CALIF.
SON

What I remember the most with my dad is the first time I wanted to shave with him. I was about 3 years old at the time. He was in the bathroom putting on shaving cream and I walked in to see what he was doing. He asked me if I also wanted to shave and with the biggest smile I said yes! He put me on the bathroom counter so I could be tall enough. My dad put shaving cream all over my face and also on my belly. He gave me a shaving razor with no razor in it. He showed me how to shave and told me to shave in those steps. After my face was done I started to shave my belly. After everything was done, he said I needed to finish by putting water on my face and belly so it wouldn't become itchy. It was one of the most exciting times I had with my dad because it was my first experience as a big kid.

MR. WILLIAM KOHN
PLACE OF BIRTH: BEAUFORT, SOUTH CAROLINA
SON

What I remember most is the many times we went fishing. This one time it was pouring down rain and I wanted to go and my dad still took me. We didn't catch a thing but it was fun.

MRS. HELEN WRIGHT
PLACE OF BIRTH: JACKSONVILLE, FLORIDA
SISTER

Uncle Buddy... The gifts you give pleases the heart of others not because of size, but because they are wrapped in love with no strings attached You are a soul that doesn't wait for happy ending's, but create them with the power of a loving heart, I'm glad the Lord blessed me with you.

MRS. MARVETTE LEONARD
PLACE OF BIRTH: JACKSONVILLE, FLORIDA
SISTER

Uncle Buddy, you are a leader who is first find solutions and last to look for problems. You have nothing to prove and nothing to defend. Just remember how special you are and how proud I am to have you as a brother. MEATHEAD

MRS. JACQUELYN ODOM
PLACE OF BIRTH: JACKSONVILLE, FLORIDA
SISTER

Aulton, the eldest of my siblings has always inspired us to live a life that's very rewarding and to stay focused on what matters the most. With his enthusiasm for like, I have no doubt his message about his life will make a difference in all areas of yours.

I am honored and humble to have been a part of his journey. To God be the glory.

MRS. CYNTHIA CHEEKS
PLACE OF BIRTH: JACKSONVILLE, FLORIDA
SISTER

All that's needs to be said is that he is my brother and I love him dearly for all he has accomplished.

MISS DEMI JONES
PLACE OF BIRTH: JACKSONVILLE, FLORIDA
GRAND DAUGHTER

The best way to predict the future is to invent it. If we do not plant knowledge when we are young, it will give us no shade as we get older. My grand dad always encourages me to continue with my education.

LaQUASHA GRAHAM
PLACE OF BIRTH: BEAUFORT, SOUTH CAROLINA
GOD DAUGHTER

I've known this man for over six years. He's been there for me, I can say for everything, I was involved in or things going on in my life. I really thank him for the wisdom he tries to pass on to me even when, at times, he doesn't know what he is talking about, but I still listen.

This man bothers me every day about my height and all I can do is laugh at him. This name I won't be able to get away from because now I'm known to everyone as TWEEIE WEENIE.

When I was a member of the Young Marines Program, I was the smallest person in the program.

We started to become close when we took a trip to the Kennedy Space Center in Florida. When all the other kids were getting ice cream, I didn't have any money, because another of the instructors was holding it for me. So I asked Mr. Kohn to borrow five dollars to buy some ice cream. I was suppose too pay him back, but I haven't and so to this day he still asks me when I'm going to pay him back.

In the last few years we have gone on trips for me to meet his family and friends. His family has taken me in as a family member, because every time you see him, you see me. Now my family considers him as my Dad. I didn't have a father growing up so he has been that father figure I needed in my life. In my eyes I always think of him as my dad. He has done more for me than I ever knew, and all the opportunities he has shown me for the future.

MISS JAIYA ALLEN
PLACE OF BIRTH: PALM COAST, FLORIDA
GOD DAUGHTER

My God-Dad always tells me I'm a leader. At 3 years old I always seem to get people to do what I want.

37

GYSGT. GREGORY WHITTAKER USMC RET.
PLACE OF BIRTH: JACKSONVILLE, FLORIDA
GOOD FRIEND

I am so thrilled that my good friend Mr. Kohn is the subject of this magnificent book. Ever since I met this great American hero he has never shown himself to be anything less than an honorable, God-fearing, outstanding individual. When I first became aware of his combat action during the Vietnam War, I was amazed and honored that God spared his life and that I was privileged with ears to hear this awesome story. I have told him on many occasions that I shared his story with everyone I make contact with. In spite of all, this great man of God and United States Marine has been through, he still manages to always greet everyone with a smile, one of his favorite saying "Hello Friend". I love you my friend and hero. May God smile upon you and your family. Semper Fi. Sir!

MISS CYNTHIA A. GOLSON
PLACE OF BIRTH: BEAUFORT, SOUTH CAROLINA
DEPUTY EEO OFFICER/ FRIEND

When I think of Mr. Kohn (as I refer to him), I think of him as a "man on a mission." He gives a lot of his time and attention to worthwhile programs. He has devoted his life to helping others and is commended for that. He is witty and loves to laugh. When Mr. Kohn in not laughing or joking with someone, then I know something is wrong. He is a man of his word and has given his all to the Marine Corps, serving as a Marine and then as a Civilian Marine. I know the Depot Museum will miss his presence. I will never forget you, Mr. Kohn. Thank you for all the Cheetos you have donated to my cause and thank you for being a great leader and friend.

Captain Stephen Christopher
Place of Birth: Memphis, Tennessee
U.S. Navy/ Dentist

Retired Gunny Sergeant Aulton Kohn is a man who enjoys life. From the first time you meet him, you can tell that he seems to enjoy whatever he's doing at the time. He has an appreciation for life, people, friends, work, and God. He seems to always be in a good mood, and he has an eternally good attitude about the challenges of life. There is always a smile on his face and always a pleasant greeting to extend to both friends and strangers. He is exactly who you want to see early in the morning because he is smiling and always has something positive to say. Gunny Kohn stays involved and active in the community and on the Marine base at Parris Island where he has many friends – there always seems to be someone that knows him no matter where he goes and they are always glad to see him. He is a shining example for people of all ages from children, to youth, to young adults, and to even us who are in middle age. Now that he is retired, I cannot imagine he will stop being involved in the community and certainly expect to see him around town and the base at Parris Island, one of the many locations where he served. He is a wonderful ambassador for the Marine Corps through which he served his nation well for many years and certainly contributes well to their espirt de corps and their proud heritage. Retired Gunny Kohn is one more superb reason the Marine Corps enjoys such an outstanding reputation for service to country and why it possesses the core values of Honor, Courage, and Commitment. He is a remarkable man, a wonderful citizen, and a shining example of how one person can make a difference in their community. All the best! Semper Fi and Godspeed

Chief Warrant Officer 4 Joseph, "JOE" Charles
Place of Birth: Fairfax, Virginia
Director IPAC: Parris Island, South Carolina

I've heard folks say that the Marine Corps teaches you how to deal with strife and hardships with your head held high, but I don't necessarily think that's true. I believe you're either born with it of you're not. The way I look at it, the Marine Corps provides opportunities (on a regular basis) where you are forced to search within yourself to fine internal strength. These are what we call our Core Values---- Honor, Courage and Commitment. Gunnery Sergeant Kohn (Mr. Al.) is the epitome of what our Core Values represent. Whether as a Marine serving in Vietnam, giving tours in the Depot Museum or showing me up in the gym every morning, he has served this great nation proudly, honorably, humbly and with a smile on his face. I consider it an honor to know him and a privilege to call him my friend.

The Rev. Dr. Sam T. Spain, Sr.
Place of Birth: Conway, South Carolina
PASTOR/FRIEND

I am the Pastor of the Lady's Island Baptist Church, Lady's Island, South Carolina. The Rev.Dr. Sam T. Spain, Sr. I am also a retired Marine Master Gunnery Sergeant, born in Conway, South Carolina. Below you will find my personal opinion of Bro. Aulton Kohn:

These words I believe describes Aulton: Courageous, discipline, a man of faith with unyielding integrity. A honest family man, one who show forth admiration for others, a modest yet humble man.

Aulton is that kind of man who will give you the shirt off his back, or lie down in a body of water for a woman to cross. An American hero without the bragging. His compassion to influence moral and spiritual truth in today's youth is noteworthy.

My prayers goes out for him as he continues to pursue "making a difference" in our society.

MRS SHARON HENDERSON-REID
Place of birth: Fort Myers, Florida
PUBLIC AFFAIRS SPECIALIST

When I think of Aulton, descriptive words like punctual, honorable, cultured, excited, delightful, helpful, friendly, capable, humorous, and goofy come into focus, and given the space, I could expand in describing my friend. I met Aulton when he was employed at the Parris Island Museum and have worked closely with him for well over 15 years. A great sense of humor. Aulton's innate ability motivates all whom he comes in contact with.

Having benefited from knowing and being around Aulton, and because of his demonstration of a "can do, will do" attitude, he also has inspired me in becoming a "motivating speaking machine." Overall, working with Aulton, I couldn't ask for a better person.

My well wishes to you Aulton in your second retirement and all who come in contact with. I know you will do yourself proud. Best of everything.

DR. STEPHEN R. WISE
PLACE OF BIRTH: TOLEDO, OHIO
DIRECTOR: PARRIS ISLAND MUSEUM

When the Depot removed the Marines from the museum and replaced them with civilians, Mr. Kohn became the first civilian guard to join the museum staff, having been spotted working in the bowling alley by Marshal Owens, the museum's assistant curator, who quickly saw that Al's people skills would be an asset to the museum. His ability to deal with people was quickly recognized by Marshal who oversaw the hiring of the new staff. Al did not disappoint. He ruled the front desk area for nearly ten years. He has the uncanny ability to spot someone chewing gum the moment they walk in the door. He was also very protective of the museum and its rules, once inviting a malcontent to step outside to settle the matter, stating that he was not as old as he looked. The situation was settled without incident. Mr. Kohn was highly sought after by tour groups and would often pose with visitors for picture opportunities. His personality added life to the opening greetings that he gave to visiting tours and he was ready to help people over the phone, especially the women. His manner and professionalism greatly enhanced the museum experience for the over one million visitors who came to the museum during his tenure.

MRS CAROLYN BRANTLEY
PLACE OF BIRTH: SAVANNAH, GEORGIA
POSTMASTER: PARRIS ISLAND/FRIEND

I met Mr. Kohn about seven years ago on Parris Island, where I worked at the post office.

Mr. Kohn is a funny person, always got jokes. One thing that I do know for sure is, Mr. Kohn is a very greedy man. He is always asking, Ms. Carolyn what do you have to eat. Another thing that I know for sure is Mr. Kohn is very cheap. Every time he comes in the post office to mail something, he will say, "Ms. Carolyn, good God almighty, it cost that much. Where is the discount and you are taking all of my lunch money!" When I see Mr. Kohn coming in the post office, I already know what he is going to say.

Overall, Mr. Kohn is a very nice gentleman. We always got along and have a good laugh with each other. I admired him for being over the Young Marines Program. Taking time out with the young people. He would come in the post office and always talked about his Young Marines, what happen over the weekend with them and trips they were going on.

I salute you Mr. Kohn, and CONGRATULATIONS on your book. I hope you much success and God continue to bless you.

MR. MOSES RILEY
PLACE OF BIRTH: YAMASSEE, SOUTH CAROLINA
FRIEND

I came in contact with Mr. Kohn at the bowling center aboard Parris Island, some years ago. We started a conversation, and it continued to grow until he became an employee at the Parris Island Museum. Just as I he is a people person, in which he started doing base tours with Discover Tours out of Hilton Head, owned by Mrs. Susan Sauser, and Mrs. Sharon Henderson Reid of the base Public Affairs Office.

There are three things that come to mind about what Mr. Kohn shared with me doing his time at the museum. "First" he really loves to "eat," secondly he would sometime stop families he never knew and fellowship with them. Third there were time he was involved in back to back to back to back presentations is just a few things that comes to mind.

MRS. TINA HEINZER
PLACE OF BIRTH: ST. LOUIS, Mo.
COMBAT FITNESS CENTER/ FRIEND

I've known Mr. Al. for a long time. He always has a smile for you. I look forward to seeing him at the fitness center every morning. Every time there was a article in The Boot newspaper I would have him signed it for me, because he is part of history. I have all his articles in a frame that he has signed. It is a honor to know him, and I hope to see my friend for a very long time.

MR. DAVE SMOOT
PLACE OF BIRTH: CALIFORNIA
FRIEND/CO-WORKER

So now I get to say things, good and bad, about Gunny Kohn

Well, there's a lot to say that's good, but I don't want to go on and on and on. Someone else can do that. I'll say just one thing: Gunny Kohn is not a boastful man even though he has a lot to boast about. Even discounting his Vietnam escapades, he has plenty to brag about. Starting the local Young Marines program and running it for years is just one example. He doesn't feel the need to prove to the world what kind of man he is. He knows it. That's enough.

And bad things? There's not many. Let's just say that if he and I are in a room with enough chow for only one, it's going to get ugly. Good fishing' Big Al.

MRS. MARY LOU BREWTON: (FRIEND)
PLACE OF BIRTH: PORTSMITH, VIRGINIA

There are Marines and then there are Marine's Marines. There is a spirit-de-corps that is personified by Gunny Kohn that, during the time that I worked with him at the Parris Island Museum, never dimmed. His enthusiasm for the USMC is worn with pride and never wavered: much like the flag he fought to protect.

EPILOGUE
IT'S OFFICIAL; WE ARE MARINES FOR LIFE

The Marine Corps' new Commandant, General James Amos, speaking at a town hall meeting declared: "A Marine is a Marine. I set that policy two weeks ago—there's no such thing as a former Marine. You're a Marine, just in a different uniform and you're in a different phase of your life. But you'll always be a Marine because you went to Parris Island, San Diego, or the hills of Quantico. There's no such thing as a former Marine.

ACKNOWLEDGMENTS

PUBLIC AFFAIR OFFICE/ PARRIS ISLAND
HUMAN RESOURCE OFFICE/ PARRIS ISLAND
MUSEUM/ PARRIS ISLAND
ARMED FORCES BANK/ PARRIS ISLAND
COMBAT FITNESS CENTER/ PARRIS ISLAND
POST OFFICE/ PARRIS ISLAND
LIBRARY/ MARINE CORPS AIR STATION, BEAUFORT

Special Thanks To:

MISS. JUNE ANDRADE—AN AUTHOR IN HER OWN RIGHT. THANKS FOR ENCOURAGING
WORDS AND MENTORING ME ON GETTING THIS PROJECT DONE.
MRS.COURTNEY DRIAZA—A SPECIAL THANK YOU FOR YOUR COMPUTER SKILLS AND
PUTTING UP WITH ME THESE PAST WEEKS.

Aulton Kohn
Gunnery Sergeant
USMC (ret)